A "Miracle" Material

by **MATTHEW KACHUR**

Table of Contents

Introduction

In 1912, the ocean liner *Titanic* crashed into an iceberg and sank in the Atlantic Ocean. When the ship was recovered in the 1990s, a vast treasure of personal objects was raised from the bottom of the sea. Among the items found were gold and silver jewelry, leather goods, coins, and ivory combs. But not a single object made of **plastic** was found!

How times have changed! Less than 100 years after the sinking of the *Titanic*, almost everything we use contains plastic. Plastic has become one of the most useful materials ever created.

Plastics are used throughout the home. The development of plastics demonstrates how chemists and engineers apply science to everyday problems, thereby making life easier.

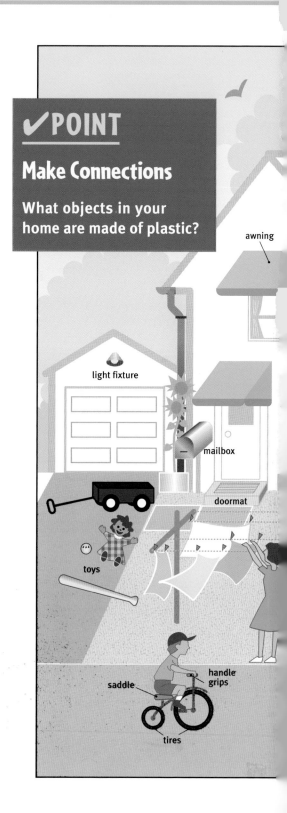

✔ **POINT**

Make Connections

What objects in your home are made of plastic?

awning

light fixture

mailbox

doormat

toys

saddle

handle grips

tires

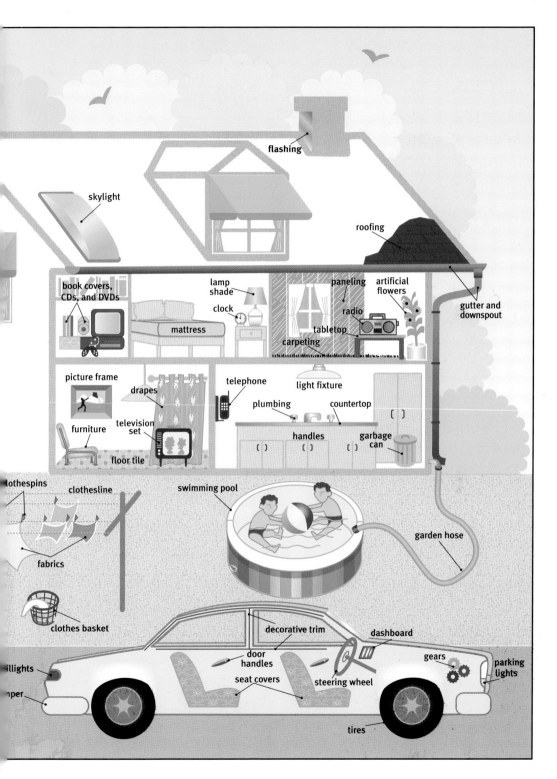

flashing

skylight

roofing

book covers,
CDs, and DVDs

lamp
shade

clock

mattress

paneling

artificial
flowers

radio

tabletop

carpeting

gutter and
downspout

picture frame

drapes

telephone

light fixture

plumbing

countertop

furniture

television
set

handles

garbage
can

floor tile

clothespins

clothesline

swimming pool

garden hose

fabrics

clothes basket

decorative trim

dashboard

door
handles

gears

parking
lights

illights

seat covers

steering wheel

mper

tires

3

The word "plastics" covers such a wide range of substances that it is not easy to say exactly what plastics are. Plastics can be hard or soft, clear or colorful, stretchy or stiff. What makes something "plastic" is that it is a **synthetic** material that can be shaped into almost any form. A synthetic material is something that does not exist in nature but is made by humans.

The word "plastic" was first written down in English in 1632. It comes from the Greek word *plastikos*, meaning "able to be molded." This is what makes plastic special. When plastic is heated and then subjected to pressure, it can be formed into almost any shape. It will keep that shape even when the heat and pressure are removed. Plastic products often last far longer than objects made of wood, paper, or glass.

We live in an age of plastics. You eat with them, play with them, and do schoolwork with them. They can be found everywhere: in homes, schools, offices, and transportation vehicles. Plastics play an important role in technology. They are part of computers and spacecraft.

Imagining a world without plastics is difficult to do. Plastics play a vital role in our lives. But many people can't decide if they love plastics or hate them. In fact, calling something "plastic" can be an insult. It means that it's fake or easily disposable.

The durability of plastics is both an advantage and a disadvantage. The fact is that although plastics can be easily thrown away, they never really go away. They do not break down as wood does.

In this book, you will learn about this "miracle" material: its history, manufacture, uses, and future.

Many sports arenas use plastic grass. Lawn decorations are also made of plastic materials.

History of Plastics

People have been making plastics for only about 200 years. However, natural substances similar to plastic have existed on Earth for a much longer time.

For many thousands of years, people made beautiful combs and jewelry out of tortoise shell, the brownish outer covering of certain sea turtles. The ancient Greeks

amber

tortoise shell

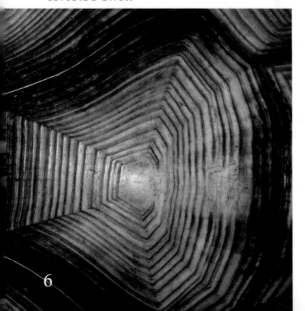

and Romans made ornaments out of amber, a fossil resin that oozed from trees that became extinct millions of years ago. And at least a thousand years ago, Europeans learned how to use shellac, another substance from trees that is similar to modern plastic, to protect wood.

All these substances have a chemical composition similar to that of plastic. But they were sometimes hard to find and the products made from them often turned brittle and broke easily.

In the 1800s, the game of billiards, sometimes called pool, became very popular. Many people wanted to play. In order to provide the ivory from which billiard balls were made, hundreds of elephants had to be killed every day. John Wesley Hyatt, a printer from Albany, New York, began to experiment with making a cheaper billiard ball. In 1869, his experiments resulted in the creation of a substance called **celluloid**. It was the first synthetic plastic.

Although celluloid did replace ivory in billiard balls, it turned out to have an even more important use. It was used to make photographic film. In the late 1800s, George Eastman advertised the use of this new film to help sell inexpensive cameras known as "Kodaks." Later, Thomas Edison punched holes in strips of celluloid and invented the motion picture, or movie.

Today, we sometimes call movie performers "celluloid stars," even though celluloid is no longer used to make film.

It's a FACT!

Hyatt's new billiard balls never became popular because they didn't make the "clicking" sound that ivory balls did. Only later was another inventor able to produce a plastic billiard ball that made that familiar sound and was generally accepted.

John Wesley Hyatt

For a while after celluloid was invented, industries could not find other useful applications for plastic. Then in 1909, Leo Baekeland, a Belgian-American chemist, invented **Bakelite**. Bakelite was the first plastic that would keep its shape under any conditions. It could be added to almost any material, including wood, and instantly made it more durable.

At about this time, chemists developed several other new types of plastic. Rayon, a form of synthetic silk, was invented in 1891. The first rayon socks and stockings were made in Germany in 1910. In 1913, the world was introduced to cellophane, the clear protective packaging layer.

Leo Baekeland

These bracelets are made of Bakelite™.

Cellophane, invented in 1924, was not waterproof at first. In 1927, scientists made the first waterproof cellophane. Notice that the bag on the right has not lost water through evaporation, as those on the left have.

New uses for plastics were developed as a result of World War II. Once war broke out in 1939, it became difficult to obtain materials such as natural rubber and silk. Rubber came from Asia and silk from Japan. Researchers began to develop plastics to replace these materials. New kinds of plastic were used to coat bullets and bomb shells, and a synthetic rubber was created for use on tanks and for the wheels of fighter planes.

When the war ended in 1945 and the economy improved, Americans were eager to purchase new things. Companies worked to develop new types of plastics. They also found new uses for old types. For example, the plastic that had been used to coat bomb shells was now used to give pots and pans a "nonstick" surface.

It's a FACT!

A week before Valentine's Day in 1946, 30,000 people mobbed the fifth floor of Gimbel's, a large New York department store. They pushed and shoved and fought to get at the merchandise. What were they after? Rare jewels? Free stuff? No, they had all come because Gimbel's had advertised that the store had 26,000 pairs of nylon stockings!

Kitchenware with nonstick coating keeps food from sticking and is easier to clean.

9

A Time Line of Plastics

The exact year in which a plastic is invented is sometimes hard to determine. Chemists often change a plastic a great deal between the time it first appears in a laboratory and the time it is available to the public. So you may find different "discovery dates" in different books.

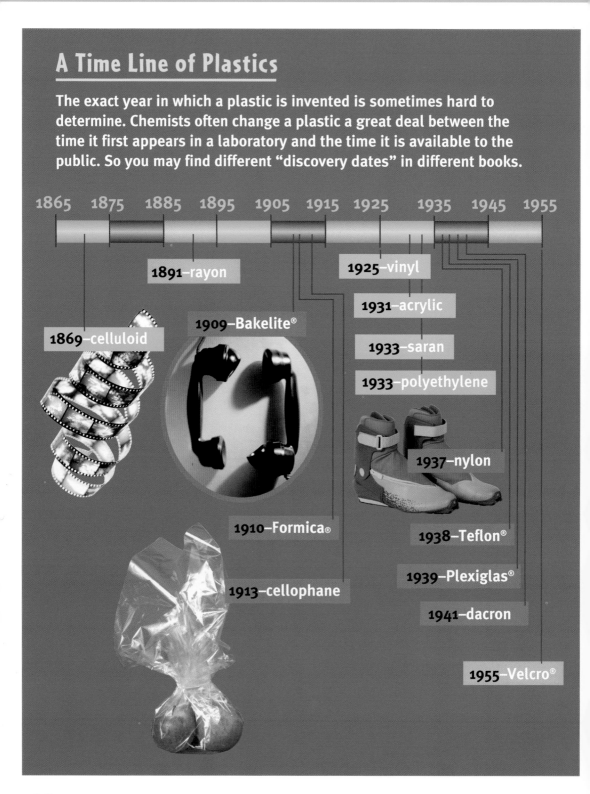

1865   1875   1885   1895   1905   1915   1925   1935   1945   1955

1891–rayon

1925–vinyl

1931–acrylic

1933–saran

1933–polyethylene

1909–Bakelite®

1869–celluloid

1937–nylon

1910–Formica®

1938–Teflon®

1939–Plexiglas®

1913–cellophane

1941–dacron

1955–Velcro®

It almost seemed as if a "miracle" plastic was invented every day between 1920 and 1960. For example, acrylic made it possible to make shatter-resistant glass, perfect for automobile windshields and eyeglasses. Polyvinyl chloride, or vinyl, was water-resistant and fire-resistant, making it just right for shower curtains, raincoats, garden hoses, and tents.

Polyethylene, discovered in 1933, became so popular that its sales totaled more than a billion pounds a year! It is now the most-used plastic product in the world. Polyethylene is used in things from dishes to baby bottles to plastic bags to artificial flowers. You know it best in plastic soda bottles, milk jugs, grocery bags, and food storage containers.

Bottles, such as these milk containers, are made of polyethylene.

1

Science of Plastics

Plastics are **polymers** (PAH-lih-merz). A polymer is a "chain" of molecules. In plastics, the polymer chains can repeat themselves millions of times. Engineers and chemists experiment with these polymer chains in the lab, changing them in various ways to make hundreds of different types of plastic.

Polymers, or giant molecules, are made by chemically combining smaller molecules known as **monomers** (MAH-nuh-merz). If just the right monomers are combined, a reaction takes place that makes the monomers cluster together, or "polymerize."

ethylene monomers

polyethylene

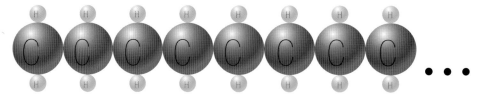

Polyethylene, a polymer, is made by chemically combining ethylene monomers to create a giant molecule.

Types of Plastics

Plastics can be divided into two categories: **thermosets** and **thermoplastics**. Thermosets can be heated and molded only once. If they are reheated, they will scorch and burn. Thermosets can tolerate high temperatures. They are used for such things as pot handles, plastic seats on buses, and various parts of airplanes and spacecraft.

Thermoplastics can be reheated and reformed again and again. This makes them relatively easy to recycle. Thermoplastics can also be mixed with liquids such as paint to produce long-lasting, high-gloss products. Most plastics are thermoplastics.

It's a FACT!

Thermosets can take as much as five minutes to set. Thermosets can be melted and molded only once.

Thermoplastics cool very quickly. Sometimes as little as ten seconds is needed to set them. Thermoplastics can be melted and remolded again and again.

13

Making and Shaping Plastics

Most plastics are made from chemicals that come from oil. A few are made from chemicals that come from natural gas, coal, cotton, and even wood. These chemicals are made into synthetic resins that are used to make plastics in the form of plastic powders. Dyes for color or glass fibers for strength can be added. The plastic powders are sold to companies that turn them into usable products.

Colorful synthetic resins, from which many kinds of plastic products are made, consist of thousands of small particles that when heated melt into a liquid much like syrup.

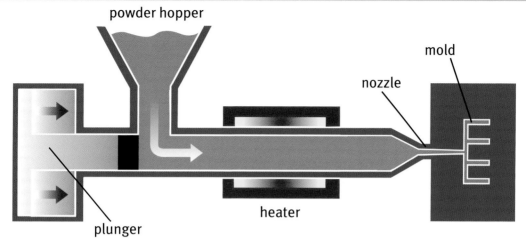

powder hopper

mold

nozzle

heater

plunger

In injection molding, plastic powder is heated and then pushed by a plunger through a nozzle into a cold mold. When the plastic is cool and rigid, the mold is opened and the object is removed.

To shape the plastic, it must first be heated until it becomes soft and runny, like maple syrup. Then the liquid plastic is shaped inside molds or hollow containers. Squeezing or injecting the soft plastic through a narrow tube into a mold is a good way to create a wide variety of plastic products. Some plastics can be squeezed through holes so tiny that the plastic comes out as fine, strong threads that can be woven into clothes. Bags are made from plastic that has been heated and rolled into thin sheets by machines with big, heavy, metal rollers.

✔POINT

Think It Over

Have you ever squeezed cake icing out of an icing tube? What happens if you put different-shaped nozzles on the bag? This is the same idea behind molding plastics.

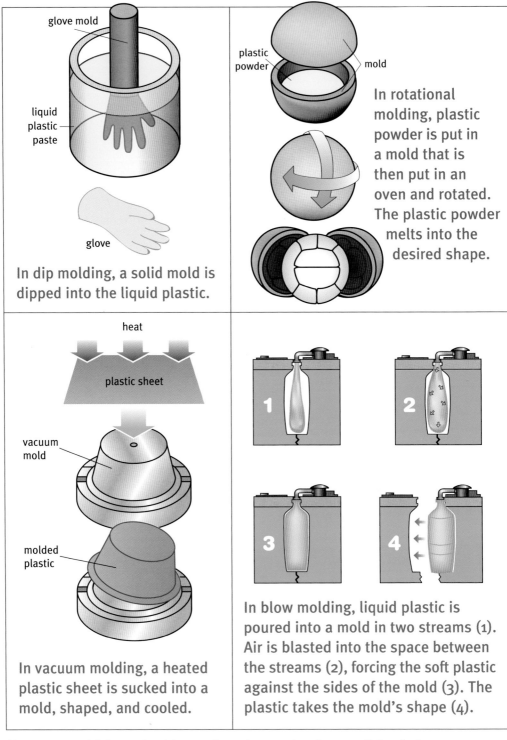

glove mold

liquid plastic paste

glove

In dip molding, a solid mold is dipped into the liquid plastic.

plastic powder

mold

In rotational molding, plastic powder is put in a mold that is then put in an oven and rotated. The plastic powder melts into the desired shape.

heat

plastic sheet

vacuum mold

molded plastic

In vacuum molding, a heated plastic sheet is sucked into a mold, shaped, and cooled.

1

2

3

4

In blow molding, liquid plastic is poured into a mold in two streams (1). Air is blasted into the space between the streams (2), forcing the soft plastic against the sides of the mold (3). The plastic takes the mold's shape (4).

No matter which method is used to shape plastic, one thing is true about all the products: When the plastic cools, it keeps its shape.

Uses of Plastics

Plastic is one of the most used and useful materials in modern life. Plastics can be found everywhere in the world, but are so common you hardly notice them at all.

Take a look at the labels inside your clothes. Do any of them say nylon or polyester? If so, you are wearing plastics. Plastics are also used for boats, automobile bodies, furniture, and building panels. Because plastics are generally very lightweight, the automobile industry depends on them to reduce the weight of cars and increase energy efficiency.

It's a FACT!

Cockleburs—a type of plant—fascinated Swiss engineer George de Mestral. The tiny burs, actually the plant's seeds, seemed impossible to get out of his clothes and his dog's fur. These stubborn burs inspired him to invent and patent the plastic hook-and-loop system known as Velcro® in 1955. The name combines parts of the French words for "velvet" and "hook."

The sleds these children use and the clothes they wear are made partially or entirely of plastic.

If you were asked to go to the store to buy "polyvinylidene chloride wrap," you would probably be confused. You wouldn't recognize that name as plastic wrap. But that's what it is, at least chemically speaking.

Years ago, people could name the items they bought as wool, cotton, iron, or wood. Most plastics, however, are known best by their brand names. You read some of these brand names on page 10. How many are you familiar with?

The plastics industry is one of the largest in the United States. In 2001, the plastics industry employed more than one million people and produced plastic products worth more than $300 billion. Plastics companies can be classified into three general groups, as the chart below shows.

Plastics Company Type	Purpose
Resin manufacturers	Companies that make and supply the chemicals to make plastics
Processors	Companies that shape the plastic powders into products
Finishers and assemblers	Companies that make plastic products by cutting, drilling, decorating, and assembling plastic parts

It is difficult to measure exactly how much plastic is produced each year because it's not simply a matter of weight or quantity of products. Plastic production is usually measured in terms of the dollar-amount value of shipments out of plastics factories. The United States, Germany, Japan, and other industrial nations lead the world in the production of plastics. The accompanying chart shows the leading states in plastic production.

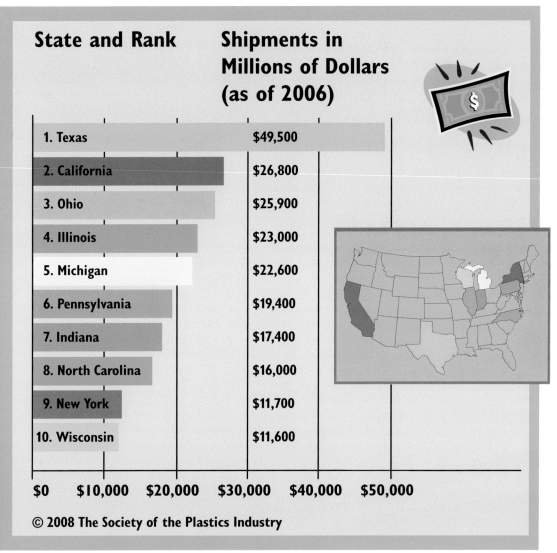

State and Rank	Shipments in Millions of Dollars (as of 2006)
1. Texas	$49,500
2. California	$26,800
3. Ohio	$25,900
4. Illinois	$23,000
5. Michigan	$22,600
6. Pennsylvania	$19,400
7. Indiana	$17,400
8. North Carolina	$16,000
9. New York	$11,700
10. Wisconsin	$11,600

$0 $10,000 $20,000 $30,000 $40,000 $50,000

© 2008 The Society of the Plastics Industry

Plastics are excellent insulators. That means they do not allow electricity or heat to pass through them easily. That's why they are used in a wide range of appliances. Many appliances, such as stoves, refrigerators, and toasters, are housed in plastic shells. Electric wires and outlets are covered in plastic. Handles of pots and pans stay cool because the plastic does not conduct heat.

This insulation property is also useful in clothing. Many people now wear thermal pants and shirts made out of plastic, and jackets filled with plastic fibers. These garments keep a person warmer than coats made with natural fibers such as cotton and wool.

Bulletproof vests are made of plastic.

Plastics are extremely versatile. That means they can be used in many different ways—and do their job well. Plastics can vary greatly in strength, from nylon stockings to bulletproof vests. They can be as soft as cotton or as rigid as steel.

Electric wires are wrapped in plastic for safety.

20

Some plastics are great at absorbing liquids. Other plastics are perfect because they don't absorb anything. Some plastics are useful because they bend, others because they don't.

Most plastics are unreactive. They will not chemically combine with other substances. This makes them excellent for storing dangerous materials, such as cleaning fluids and insecticides.

These plastic bottles are useful because they neither absorb the liquids they contain nor react with them.

The driver behind the wheel of this car avoided being cut by glass because the windshield was made of shatter-resistant plastic.

Plastics have almost completely replaced wood and metal as the main material in children's toys. Plastic is lighter, cheaper, and more unbreakable. It doesn't give splinters and its colors don't come off. Some of the most popular toys today are made out of plastic.

Silly Putty, a type of plastic first marketed in 1949, sold faster than any toy in history until that time. Its sales for the first year were $6 million. At the height of the hula-hoop craze in 1957, plastic hoop sales topped $15 million. A factory in California made 20,000 plastic hula hoops every day using more than a million pounds of polyethylene.

It's a FACT!

Frisbees are little more than plastic pie tins that look like a pizza crust. But since their introduction in 1957, more than 200 million of them have been sold.

High-density polyethylene is harder and less flexible than regular polyethylene. It was first used to make hula hoops, a fad in the 1950s.

Plastics as Art

Some artists, known as pop (for "popular") artists, enjoy working with plastic. They try to combine the kind of art found in museums with ordinary objects that everyone knows.

✔POINT

Make Connections

Look at the picture on this page. Have you seen this type of art before? What is your opinion of pop art?

Christo, a Bulgarian-American pop artist, used 1,067,330 square feet (99,155 square meters) of nylon fabric and 60 miles (96.5 km) of vinyl tube to create "The Gates" installation in Central Park in 2005.

23

Future of Plastics

In the year 2000, Americans produced more than 200 million tons of garbage compared to 88 million tons in 1960. That is almost 4.5 pounds (2 kilograms) of waste per person per day, up from 2.7 pounds (1.2 kilograms) per person per day only forty years ago. Much of the increased garbage was in the form of plastics.

Plastics are specially designed to be long-lasting and durable. These qualities are advantageous when the plastics are being used. But when the plastics are ready to be discarded, problems arise. Plastics do not decay. So as more and more people use plastics, more and more waste is produced. Millions of tons of plastic products accumulate in landfills as waste and contribute to environmental **pollution.**

To make matters worse, plastics are difficult to burn. They clog incinerators and emit harmful fumes.

TRY THIS!

1. Have an adult help you with this activity. Bury some paper products (cups, bags) and some plastic products near one another. Mark the spot.

2. Come back in three weeks and dig up the objects. Check on the objects several more times during the year. Does the plastic disappear?

Recycling is one of the best ways to prevent Earth from filling up with plastic garbage. In the 1970s, many cities and towns began recycling programs as a way to get rid of consumer waste. These communities encouraged citizens to sort and clean plastic items, such as soda bottles and milk jugs, and bring them to a recycling center or put them at the curb of the street for pickup. Recycling efforts became very popular and continue to be today.

The number of businesses involved in recycling plastics tripled between 1990 and 2000. More than 1,700 U.S. businesses now recycle and reclaim plastics. New uses for recycled plastic products grow every day. Recycling plastics instead of burning them also helps reduce the greenhouse gases that cause global warming.

It's a FACT!

About 30 percent of plastic bottles are now recycled into other useful objects.

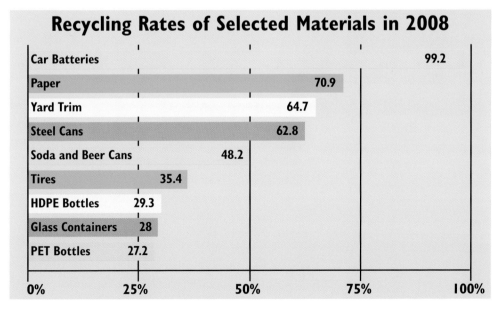

Recycling Rates of Selected Materials in 2008

Material	Rate
Car Batteries	99.2
Paper	70.9
Yard Trim	64.7
Steel Cans	62.8
Soda and Beer Cans	48.2
Tires	35.4
HDPE Bottles	29.3
Glass Containers	28
PET Bottles	27.2

0%   25%   50%   75%   100%

Recycling is not limited to a community effort. It is an individual effort, too. You can do something about plastic pollution!

You can avoid buying items that use wasteful packaging, such as individually wrapped slices of cheese and overly wrapped CDs. You can recycle all plastic materials you and your family use, such as food containers and drink bottles.

You can also try to convince your neighbors to care more about plastic waste. In the late 1980s, U.S. schoolchildren played a crucial role in forcing a fast-food company to stop using plastic foam shells for their hamburgers. The students launched a huge Send-It-Back campaign in which they returned the plastic packaging to the company executives. The company finally agreed to get rid of the foam packaging.

PLASTIC CODE SYSTEM FOR PLASTIC CONTAINERS

CODE		MATERIAL	TYPICAL PRODUCTS
1	PETE	Polyethylene terephthalate	Soda bottles
2	HDPE	High density polyethylene	Milk and water jugs
3	PVC	Polyvinyl chloride	Plumbing pipes
4	LDPE	Low density polyethylene	Bread bags
5	PP	Polypropylene	Yogurt containers
6	PS	Polystyrene	Foam cups, egg cartons
7	OTHER	All other resins	Ketchup bottles

A coding system identifies the type of plastic used. This is helpful to consumers as well as processing plants that recycle plastic objects.

✔POINT

Talk About It

Choose the photo that represents what you want for your future. Talk to a group member about ways to make the photo a reality.

WE RECYCLE

In the 1970s, scientists first introduced **biodegradable** plastics, which are plastics that break down when they are consumed, or eaten, by bacteria. Scientists also created **photodegradable** plastics that break down when they are exposed to sunlight.

Although biodegradeable plastics would be excellent for the environment, the first generation of these plastics didn't work out as expected. So chemists are continuing their research into making plastic products that are truly biodegradable. When their efforts are successful, plastic products will be 100 percent disposable. They will not be a source of pollution.

The biodegradable plastic fork decomposes completely in 45 days.

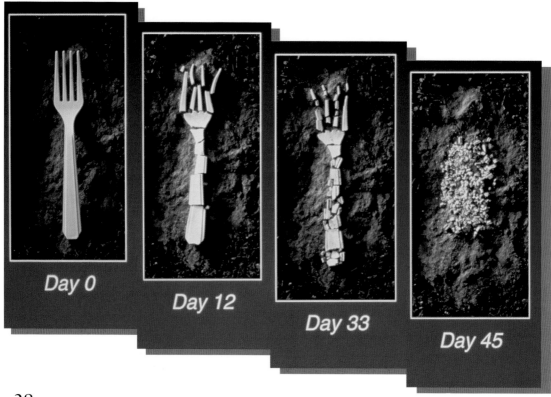

Day 0

Day 12

Day 33

Day 45

It's a FACT!

The Jarvik 7, the world's first artificial plastic heart, was implanted in Barney Clark by surgeon William DeVries in 1982.

Plastics allow doctors to replace body parts that have been lost or have worn out and no longer function properly.

Synthetic limbs are another important medical application of plastics.

Will some new "miracle" plastic be invented this year? It's always hard to see into the future, but many scientists believe that important new plastics are unlikely to be developed anytime soon. Instead, chemists are now working on improving the plastics that already exist. Some of the most exciting research developments involve the use of fillers, such as wood flour or flax, to extend the life and improve the quality of plastics.

Some plastics can conduct electricity very well. Recent discoveries have made this ability even more powerful. Other plastics have been developed that can stand super-high temperatures, such as those in an engine. The demand for plastics keeps increasing steadily, so one can only wonder about what the future will bring.

29

You have just read about how scientific knowledge improved many aspects of life with the development of plastics. You also know how plastics are made and what they are used for.

In the last thirty years, plastics have appeared in thousands of products. Scientists keep finding new uses for plastics in medicine, nuclear and space research, industry, and architecture.

The development of plastics into a major industry is a great human achievement story. But we must be sure that in our quest for a better life, we do not pollute the environment and cover Earth with garbage. Plastics are amazing substances, but only humans can make wise decisions about what is right for the future of our home planet, Earth.

The Millennium Dome, in Greenwich, England, is the largest synthetic fabric structure in the world. The roof of the Dome covers 20 acres and is so strong it could support the weight of a jumbo jet.

Glossary

Bakelite	(BAY-keh-lite) the first synthetic thermosetting plastic, discovered in 1909 (page 8)
biodegradable	(by-oh-dih-GRAY-duh-bul) capable of being decomposed by bacteria and other biological agents (page 28)
celluloid	(SEL-yuh-loid) a colorless synthetic plastic formerly used in making photographic film, discovered in 1869 (page 7)
monomer	(MAH-nuh-mer) a smaller molecule chemically combined to make a polymer (page 12)
photodegradable	(foh-toh-dih-GRAY-duh-bul) capable of being decomposed by exposure to sunlight (page 28)
plastic	(PLAS-tik) a synthetic material that is soft and easily shaped when heated but hard when cooled (page 2)
pollution	(puh-LOO-shun) contamination of Earth's air, water, and land (page 24)
polyethylene	(pah-lee-EH-thih-leen) a plastic used especially for containers, tubes, and packaging (page 11)
polymer	(PAH-lih-mer) a type of natural or synthetic chemical compound, formed by simple molecules linked together into giant molecules (page 12)
recycling	(ree-SY-kul-ing) the re-use of materials like plastic for new purposes (page 25)
synthetic	(sin-THEH-tik) something not of natural origin (page 4)
thermoplastic	(ther-muh-PLAS-tik) a plastic that can be reheated and reset over and over again (page 13)
thermoset	(THER-moh-set) a plastic that can be heated and set only once (page 13)

Index